I War

MW01224799

by Dominic O'Grady
illustrated by Dona Turner

Harcourt
SCHOOL PUBLISHERS

Copyright © by Harcourt, Inc.

All rights reserved. No part of this publication may be reproduced or transmitted in any form or by any means, electronic or mechanical, including photocopy, recording, or any information storage and retrieval system, without permission in writing from the publisher.

Requests for permission to make copies of any part of the work should be addressed to School Permissions and Copyrights, Harcourt, Inc., 6277 Sea Harbor Drive, Orlando, Florida 32887–6777. Fax: 407-345-2418.

HARCOURT and the Harcourt Logo are trademarks of Harcourt, Inc., registered in the United States of America and/or other jurisdictions.

Printed in China

ISBN 10: 0-15-358452-1
ISBN 13: 978-0-15-358452-7

Ordering Options
ISBN 10: 0-15-358357-6 (Grade K Above-Level Collection)
ISBN 13: 978-0-15-358357-5 (Grade K Above-Level Collection)
ISBN 10: 0-15-360689-4 (package of 5)
ISBN 13: 978-0-15-360689-2 (package of 5)

If you have received these materials as examination copies free of charge, Harcourt School Publishers retains title to the materials and they may not be resold. Resale of examination copies is strictly prohibited and is illegal.

Possession of this publication in print format does not entitle users to convert this publication, or any portion of it, into electronic format.

4 5 6 7 8 9 10 0940 15 14 13 12 11 10 09

I toss the bag.
I want to hit the can.
If I hit it, I will win.

I am sad, Mom and Dad.
I did not hit the can.
I did not win the top.

I want the cup to go up.
I want to win the doll.

I am sad.
The cup did not go up.
I did not win the top.
I did not win the doll.

I did not win the top.
I did not win the doll.
What can I do to win.

You can do this.
Look at what you can win!
You can do it!

I did it!
I got two little ducks.
I got a big, big dog!